Not Tonight, Darling, I Have A Headache!

365 WAYS TO WEASEL YOUR WAY OUT OF SEX

by

Marie Chablis & Addie Michel

Published by

Laughing Venus™

www.laughingvenus.com

First Printing, November, 2008
Second Printing, June 2009

ISBN 978-0-615-31156-2

Illustrations by Drew Krevi · www.drewkreviart.com
Art Direction by Michael Woolf · myartdirector@gmail.com

Forward

Laughing Venus is dedicated to supporting and enhancing female friendships.

Not Tonight, Darling, I Have a Headache!
365 Ways to Weasel Your Way Out of Sex
is a humorous book that is sure to stimulate conversation and generate a night full of laughs while out with the girls.

Disclaimer

Girls, it should go without saying,
but we still think it's a good idea to remind
you... please take these ideas in the spirit
in which they are intended. These are funny
thoughts to generate laughs and good times
with your girlfriends.

Please use common sense if you
actually desire to put
any of these into practice.

Just as an example,
don't actually bring the bee to bed!

A Note from the Authors

Not Tonight, Darling, I Have a Headache!
365 Ways to Weasel Your Way Out of Sex
was inspired by numerous conversations
we had with girlfriends over
a glass of wine or a great meal.

We were compelled to write this book because
we felt most women could identify with and
find humor in the subject matter.

It is our desire that it will be shared with
friends in a lighthearted manner and
that laughter will ensue.

Enjoy!

Acknowledgements

Thanks to our wonderful, loving husbands
who, despite the subject matter, supported our
vision to create a humorous reference book that
enhances our female friendships.

Their feedback with respect to content
was taken into consideration
- but ultimately rejected -
and their suggestion to publish
this book under pen names
was well received and agreed upon.

We treasure the multitude of girlfriends
we have in our life and appreciate the fun,
unique and unexpected suggestions they
provided for the book.

Finally, thank you to our fantastic art team:
Drew Krevi, who provide us with these
incredibly inspired illustrations and
Michael Woolf who gave us Drew
(and, as our art director,
fashioned our newly polished look).

FIRST
THINGS
FIRST

Let's face it...
we all share in the sisterhood of the
modern day Venus. Of course,
we're goddesses of love and beauty,
and of course our man can't resist us.

But unlike the Venus of love, we live
in the twenty-first century,
so in addition to our "love duties,"
we also need to manage the kid activities,
ace the big work presentation,
grab the groceries, prepare (sometimes)
nutritious gourmet meals,
plant the spring pots,
and on and on and on.

It's pretty clear: with our busy lives,
something's got to give.

Any guesses?

That something tends to be at
The end of the day, when we're really
tired from our crazy schedule.

We can always do that something tomorrow.

That something starts with an S and falls
somewhere down the list of nighttime
S priorities, well behind sleep.

Following the S is an
E standing for every.

Every time you're drifting off into
la la land, you can count on your
partner being ready to romp.

Every time you think you've snuck into
bed without awakening him, ping!

Every woman we know understands
what we're talking about.

X, the last letter in this word,
stands for excuse.

That's where this book comes in.

We all love our partners, and maybe to their
surprise, we actually do enjoy sex.
And yes, we could barely wait to
jump into bed when we first met.

But as the years went on we became
well aware of the fact that our man's
sexual appetite was a bit larger than ours,
and quite frankly, most nights we just
want to go to sleep!

Do we really need to read another book
on how to ignite the spark,
rekindle the romance,
or find our passion?

No!

What we do need is a simple little
book telling women what they
really want to know:

How can I get into bed tonight
without arousing my partner?

We've all been there...
stalled in the bath, read a magazine
until we think he's asleep,
claimed sheer exhaustion, right?

FIRST THINGS FIRST

Speaking of exhaustion, you may have
exhausted many of your tried and
true excuses, and that's where this
book can really help.

We're here to present fresh,
new ideas to eke out one more night of
undisturbed relaxation.

Here we go!

CHAPTER 1
SET THE MAN STRAIGHT

Does your sweetie constantly rely on these
"self-recorded" statistics that
so-and-so is doing "it" eight times a week,
or this guy gets a blowjob every time
his wife has her period?

Well... here are a few statistics
we've found that you may want to be
ready to pull out of your mental bank:

Married couples make love a robust
98 times per year, while single folks are
having sex only 49 times a year.
He should consider himself
lucky he's married!

12% of couples in America don't even
sleep in the same room. Again, tell him to
consider himself lucky —

he could be on the couch!

57% of people say they have sex
at least once per week.

So let him know you may be a
bit short, but well within the norm.

The average couple in their
forties has sex 69 times a year
(no pun intended!).

The average couple in their
thirties reportedly does it
86 times a year.

The average couple in their twenties
does it 112 times a year—
positive proof that one gets
wiser with age.

4% of respondents to a survey
claim to have sex daily.
Certainly no one we know.

People around the world would
rather go out with their friends
than have sex.

More than one-fifth of people
chose spending time with their peers
rather than having sex with a partner,
while another 10% prefer either to
play sports or to go shopping.

See, I am normal!
Now where was that sale?

Now that you're armed and dangerous
with your own version of sexual reality,
it's time to lay the ground rules in
your relationship.

CHAPTER 2
LAY THE GROUND RULES

It's important to set expectations up front.

Defining the ground rules helps your man understand when he can and cannot initiate sex.

Once established, if he can find a time that is acceptable to initiate sex, let him go for it.

You'll have plenty of outs!

Ground Rules — simply tell him...

"HONEY, THERE WILL BE NO SEX..."

1) in the middle of the night, once I've fallen asleep

2) once you've fallen asleep

3) if you roll over and say,
"Do you want to fool around?"

"HONEY, THERE WILL BE NO SEX..."

4) if you roll over and say,
"Do you want to make love?"

5) for twelve weeks (at least) after having a baby

6) involving an alternate hole

"HONEY, THERE WILL BE NO SEX..."

7) if you're lying in bed naked and waiting for it

8) if you're drunk

9) if you fart under the covers

"HONEY, THERE WILL BE NO SEX..."

10) without foreplay/romance

11) if you rub up against me like a pervert

12) if you mention it earlier in the day

"HONEY, THERE WILL BE NO SEX..."

13) if I have my period or
am expecting it that night

14) if the kids are awake

15) if you piss me off earlier in the evening

"HONEY, THERE WILL BE NO SEX..."

16) if I've overeaten and feel bloated

17) if you wake me up early
in the morning to have sex

18) when we have overnight guests

"HONEY, THERE WILL BE NO SEX..."

19) if we're in our parent's house

20) if the kids have an overnight guest

21) if the kids are sick

Given the way men tend to operate,
these ground rules alone should help
you weasel you way out of sex
up to 20% of the nights,
buying you immediate slumber
for 73 nights of the year!

Free Passes

Without a doubt, every woman deserves
a minimum of one free pass per month...
no questions asked.

This buys you twelve additional nights of slumber.

(FREE PASS noted throughout book)

CHAPTER 3
SET THE TONE EARLY IN THE DAY

There are little "things" that you can do
during the day to increase your odds of success
at weaseling your way out of sex.

An ounce of prevention goes a long way.

Here are just a few examples:

22) Tell your husband that if he does the laundry,
makes dinner, cleans the kitchen,
gives the kids a bath, reads to each child individually,
and puts the kids to bed, you'll have sex.

He'll fall asleep!

23) Mention, as he heads out the door for work,
that you've noticed he has some early signs of
dementia, i.e. forgetfulness.

That night climb into bed and tell him that
even though you thoroughly enjoyed your
sex last night, twice, and this morning,
you now need your sleep.

Oh... did he forget?

"Bring out that large bag of new clothes..."
(Excuse #51)

24) Power-shop all day and leave
the receipts and shopping bags all over the house.

Do this on the day you get your credit card bill.

This will surely lead to a lecture, argument, and
your refusal to have sex on the grounds
he doesn't support your passion.

25) Get up early in the morning to make a
pan of gourmet laxative brownies to
pack in his lunch for dessert.

Be sure to send a couple of extra
for a mid-afternoon snack.

26) A good Feng Shui bedroom
promotes sensual energy.

Create an anti-Feng Shui environment in your
bedroom by filling it with your TV
computer, and exercise equipment,
close all windows to keep fresh air out,
have only bright can lights installed,
paint your bedroom a shockingly bright color,
place sad and lonely pictures on the wall,
push two sides of the bed up against a wall and
place bed in direct line of the door, have only
one bedside table and keep all doors open at night.

It may also help to leave clothes lying all over the floor.
He may trip and get too irritated to perform.
Admittedly, most men won't care if the room is
void of "sensual energy"—
so refer to the other ideas in this book if needed!

If you fail to set the tone during the day,
you'll be forced to move onto
Plan B: Stalling Techniques.

CHAPTER 4
STALLING TECHNIQUES

Stalling techniques are suggested
methods to kill time while waiting for
your partner to fall asleep.

If he wakes up,
default to Ground Rule #2.

27) Lie with your child to
help them "get to sleep"...
of course you could
accidentally fall asleep yourself.

28) Finish your novel.

29) Pull out the old douche kit and enjoy.

30) Color-code the files in your file drawer.

31) Dust the chandelier.

32) Clean up a few e-mails.

33) Organize your closet.

34) Use Google® to seek out potential vacation spots for spring break.

35) Shop eBay®.

36) Fold those three loads of laundry that have been lying next to the dryer forever.

37) Speed-dial a girlfriend on the phone,
then talk for an hour.

38) Organize the junk drawer;
we all know that will take until morning!

39) Polish the silver—
haven't you been meaning to get to that?

40) Organize the recyclables.

41) Have a venti, triple shot, half soy, quarter mocha, part skim latte.

42) Call your sister.

43) Finish off that bottle of wine.

44) Buy him a new video game and
have him try it out before bed.

45) Replace the batteries in the smoke detectors.

"Fold those three loads of laundry..."
(Excuse #36)

46) Have a midnight snack.

47) Play "hide and seek" and hide
in a really good place.
Eventually he'll give up and go to bed.

48) Ask him to run to the grocery store to
pick up some feminine pads for you.

49) Watch your TiVo® shows.

50) Get everything ready for your
"early" business meeting tomorrow:
iron clothes, polish shoes, polish jewelry,
paint nails... as one thing leads to another,
you'll be cleaning out all of the old shoe polish and
sorting through your entire jewelry chest.

51) Bring out that large bag of new clothes
you've been hiding and insist on
trying everything on for him, including
every combination that would work from
your closet with these new clothes.

52) Catch up on a celebrity gossip magazine.

53) Take a long route home from
dropping off the babysitter...
in fact, consider house hunting.

54) FREE PASS

55) Whiten your teeth.

56) Replace any burned out light bulbs.

57) Discuss how adorable the new lawn boy is, especially his six pack abs.

58) Talk about his ex. Does he still think about her, does he compare you to her, it hurts to think he may, even if he says he doesn't the thought still hurts.

59) Ask him how many partners he's had
and casually mention that you've
had more but don't want to talk about it.

60) Tell him you've been waiting all week
to see a certain person on Jay Leno
tonight and don't want to be distracted.

61) Do an enema in bed, hop on the toilet,
and yell to him that you need to wait
until it all drains out.

62) Pop in a Do Not Disturb (DND)
bath bomb and relax in the bath
for a couple of hours.

63) Call a girlfriend to discuss your
peculiar vaginal discharge.

64) Tell him he needs to shower first.

"Call your sister..."
(Excuse #42)

65) Text incessantly.

66) Watch a "tear jerker" movie
and bawl in bed.

67) Play your new Wii™ exercise game...
not in the bedroom, for obvious reasons.

---

68) Call a girlfriend while in bed to discuss what a "normal" penis size is.

70) Do a manicure and pedicure and tell him you need to wait for your nails to dry.

69) Do the extra hard Sudoku® puzzle in today's paper.

---

71) Tell him you need to do 250 Kegel reps
to tighten that area for next time.

72) Tell him you just did a suppository
and need to wait until it's absorbed.

73) Be nostalgic and work on a Rubik's Cube®.

74) Do your nightly meditation and repeat "ohm"
quietly at first, then progressively louder,
for about two hours.

Tell him if he interrupts you, you'll have to start over.

75) Mention that he ripped you last time with his large
manhood and you need a few days to heal.

If stalling techniques aren't producing the results you're
looking for, you need to take more drastic measures.

Consider the following techniques to physically
turn him off so he won't even want to have sex...
perhaps ever again!

CHAPTER 5
TURN-OFF
TACTICS

Turn-off tactics are your "nuts" and "screws"
(no pun intended) to get out of sex.

PHYSICAL TURN-OFFS

Some physical turn-offs will require
a Turn-Off Prop (TOP).

76) Body odor —
throw the deodorant out the window.

77) Come out of the bathroom with toilet paper
hanging out of your panties or jammies.

78) Halitosis — eat roasted garlic right before bed and breathe on him, or let your mouth get very stale and sleep on his chest, gazing up at him with your mouth open, exhaling a sigh of contentment.

79) Big bushy bush.

(TOP #1—a faux piece of fur applied to the pubic area).

80) Have explosive diarrhea in the master bath before bed.

(TOP #2—a laxative or gas-producing dinner)

81) Wear a pair of Depends™ to bed and say,
"Sorry... I'm experiencing incontinence".

(TOP #3 – an adult diaper)

82) Nipple hair.

(TOP #4 — individual false eyelashes —
attach single lashes to nipple or areola to create breast hair).

83) Nose hair.

(TOP #4 — attach single lashes to the
inside of nose, creating visible nose hair)

84) Chin hair.

(TOP #4 — attach multiple lashes to
the chin area creating a beard)

85) Mustache.

(TOP #4 — attach single lashes to
edge of mouth creating a girl "stache")

86) Place an extra large dildo,
enhanced with hair, on his pillow.

(TOP #5 – an extra large dildo)

87) FREE PASS

88) Leave yeast infection medication on the nightstand.

(TOP #6—yeast infection medication)

FYI.... Yeast infections can last for a month or so.

89) Fake a period stain in the bed.

(TOP #8 — mix red food coloring with corn syrup)

90) Wear a pair of large granny underwear to bed.

(TOP #9 — an old pair of your mother-in-law's underwear)

91) Clip your toenails in bed.

92) Wear a pair of underwear with a string
hanging out of the bottom.

(TOP #10 — a pair of full bottom underwear with
small rope attached signifying a very heavy period!)

"Pre-record a kid's crying on your cell phone..."
(Excuse #52)

93) Wear a long, braided pubic hair extension to bed.

(TOP #11 — a long piece of faux hair attached to
your pubic area by microscopic clips)

94) Leave an ovulation kit on the nightstand.

(TOP #12 — a digitized ovulation kit with five sticks
laying out, one stick used to show you're serious).

95) Place bladder infection antibiotics on the nightstand.

(TOP #7 — an old antibiotic bottle with
vitamins inside — he'll never look!)

96) Put a framed picture of the parents/in-laws on the nightstandand mention how much you miss them.

97) Place a Rosie O'Donnell photo on nightstand.

98) Come to bed with hair/food stuck in your teeth.

99) Leave an MD script pad with the words "highly infectious" written on it.

(TOP #13 — MD script pad)

100) Fake an extended case of hiccups.

101) Do an all night mud mask before bed.

102) Fake snoring.

103) Fake farting.

(TOP #14 — Whoopie Cushion — place under your buttocks and continue to roll onto it)

104) Get into bed and put on a C-PAP machine for sleep apnea. Your man will think he's sleeping with an alien.

105) Place hemorrhoid cream on the nightstand.

(TOP #15 — bottle of Preparation H®)

106) Bleach your mustache.

107) Push out some really bad gas.

108) Reverse-tweeze your brow by taking TOP #4 and filling in the area between your brows to cause a unibrow.

109) Develop a tick.

110) Apply a faux canker sore.

(TOP #16 — one of your kid's Halloween tattoos that resembles an oozing sore)

111) Drop a log in the master bathroom just before bed and forget to flush.

112) Fish oil body smell.

(TOP #17 — rub contents from a bottle of fish sauce on your inner thighs)

113) Pretend to squeeze pimples on the inside of your thighs and buttocks in bed.

114) Shave the bush quickly before bed, then place bandages all over the pubic area.

115) Leave a huge maxi pad on the bed.

116) Wear the same panties all week.

117) Pick a booger... and if desperate, eat it.

118) Get into bed with dingleberries
(toilet paper balls) hanging from your bush.

119) Eat tons of beans for dinner,
creating a distended stomach in addition to gas.

120) FREE PASS

121) Put a raisin in your nose to develop a nose whistle.

122) Don't shave your arms/legs for a month.

"Catch up on a celebrity gossip magazine..."
(Excuse #52)

123) Ask him if he'll check to see if your anal warts
have shrunk since applying meds, or ask him
if he wants you to check his rear for anal warts.

124) Go to bed with a milk mustache.

125) Put a smelly baby diaper on the bed.

126) Eat asparagus for dinner and
pee in the master bathroom before bed.

127) Relocate the cat's litter box to under your bed.

128) Dye your entire pubic hair area gray and ask
your man if he thinks you're getting a
couple of stray strands of gray hair "down there."

129) Read a book in bed about how to conceive after forty.

130) Offer to massage his genital area
and accidently grab the Icy Hot®.

131) Ask him to be careful not to touch your hernia bump.

132) Apply skid marks to your underwear using a dark chocolate bar.

133) Come out of the bathroom "stringing" your egg white ovulation mucus between your fingers.

134) Ask him if he'll insert a suppository for you before bed.

135) Wear men's underwear to bed —
though this may be a turn on to some men.

136) Wear an extra large menstrual pad that sticks
out of the front and back of your underwear.

137) Wear "old fashion" hair rollers and a robe to bed.

138) Place a wood tick in your pubic hair and ask your man to pull it out.

MEDICAL TURN-OFFS:

Keep this book by your bed to be used as a quick reference
for signs and symptoms that help you fake
an illness with confidence.

Illness requires plenty of rest and time to recover.
Any energy expended doing an unnecessary act will take
away from your body's ability to heal!

Remember to over-exaggerate and visualize that
Oscar®-winning performance!

Here are some tid bits of information
to help you accomplish your goal:

139) Appendicitis — pain in the middle of your belly.

140) Gall stone — indigestion and pain in the upper right part of your belly.

141) Kidney stone — stabbing pain in the side and back below the ribs that tends to come in waves.

142) Strep throat — throat pain
(Highly Contagious: Do not lay facing
your man, let alone do the act!).

143) Ringworm — small, red circles or ovals all over
your body. These can be made easily with a red pen.

144) Flu — pain in your back, arms and legs,
headache and fatigue...

How many of us don't have at least
one of these symptoms daily anyway?

145) Abscessed tooth — pain in jaw,
horrible smelling mouth.

146) Pink eye — put a layer of honey
below your eye (not in it!)

147) Asthma attack — heavy wheezing.
Sit down halfway up the steps,
take deep breaths, and tell him you need to rest.

148) Chicken pox — small fluid filled
blisters on face and trunk.

(Give yourself small hickies all over your body,
put drops of oil on a few and tell him you were exposed).

149) Earache — point to your left ear and
tell him you have severe ear pain.

If necessary, drip some honey near your earlobe.

CAUTION: Do not apply honey to any
other part of your body!

150) PMS — mood changes, irritability,
fluid retention, bloated stomach, tender breasts.

151) Herpes — pain, tenderness or itchy sensation,
blisters, or open sores.

152) Yeast infection — itching and irritation
of the vagina, thick white discharge.

153) Herniated disk — sore neck,
intense pain in your back,
burning pain down one or both legs.

154) Food Poisoning — severe abdominal pain.

MENTAL TURN-OFFS

If your man is rip-roarin' and ready to go,
mental turn-off techniques may squelch his libido.

155) Make the statement,
"I'll lay here, just get it over with."

156) Blurt out the wrong name.

157) Put in a Dick Does Dan
porno movie to watch together.

158) Talk to your man in baby talk:
"Mommy's going to..."

159) Suggest starting with a very large dildo and
then have your partner "finish it up."
(TOP #5).

160) FREE PASS

161) Suggest "talking about your feelings" before sex.

162) Name your body parts after your in-laws.

163) Say, "Let's make a baby."

164) Mention a story you think you heard on the news
regarding a new sexually transmitted disease
that you can get from toilet seats and that
you may have some of the symptoms.

"Eat an entire box of Oreo® cookies..."
(Excuse #184)

165) Tell him your IUD fell out today...
you can still make love, but you may get pregnant.

166) Hand him a bottle of Dude Lube™
and tell him to take care of it himself.

167) Tell him your period is late.

168) Mention that you have a gynecologic appointment
tomorrow and are worried the doctor will be
able to tell that you just had sex.

169) Stick an annoying, repetitive musical toy in the bed
that is set off by motion or voice.

170) Slip into a hand-me-down outfit from
your mother and tell him that evidently
this outfit really turned his father-in-law on.

171) Have a talk about money,
renovation projects, etc., before sex.

172) Tell your man you've decided to pick up the guitar and
sit in bed practicing and singing, "Blowin' in the Wind"
over and over again until you get it perfect.

CAUTION: Use of the word "blow" in any context is risky.

173) Ask him how long he thinks it will take.

174) Let out a few big sighs.

175) Start sobbing about something a friend told you today.

176) Lay there despondent and fake depression.

177) Let him initiate and immediately ask him,
"Are you done yet?"

178) Have a talk about differences in parenting styles.

179) Bring up your father/mother-in-law.

180) Sing the National Anthem while
laying next to him in bed.
Anything for your country.

181) Send subliminal messages
(turn away and curl into fetal position).

182) Comment on the article you just read on large penises and ask if you can measure his.

183) Casually say, "I just know I'm ovulating."

184) Eat an entire box of Oreo® cookies while laying next to him (and the crumbs) in bed, and then smile.

185) Hand him a doctor's prescription stating you must abstain from sex for six weeks due to inactive vaginal muscles.

(TOP #13 — MD script pad)

186) Pinch the "spare tire" around his waist and mention that you're going to hold on for the ride.

CAUTION: He may just say okay.

TURN-OFF TACTICS

187) Tell him something that irritates
him and kills the mood.

188) Ask him if you can squeeze that zit on his back first.

189) Tell him you need to lose just
five more pounds and you'll be in the mood.

190) Suggest listening to Barry Manilow
music during foreplay.

CAUTION: he may like it...
but then you have bigger issues.

191) Mention that you just got notification of a lice
breakout in school and your bush feels itchy.

"Play hide and seek..."
(Excuse #47)

192) Pull out a box of extra-small condoms and say that you special ordered them for him.

193) Tell him you're still trying to figure out what that inchworm you dug up today in the garden reminds you of.

194) Lay a brochure on the bed that
talks about penile enlargement procedures.

195) Tell him you'd rather work off the
one or two calories you'd expend tomorrow.

196) Mention how much he reminds you of his father.

197) Get your child's recorder instrument and
tell your man you want him to listen to you practice
playing "Bridge Over Troubled Water" until you
get it perfect for the kindergarten graduation ceremony.

Explain that you need to do this in bed once the kids
have gone to sleep, because you want it to be
a surprise for little "Tommy."

198) Laugh uncontrollably... and if you can, fart.

199) Mention the doctor appointment you made for him to have an annual rectal exam followed by a colonoscopy.

200) Ask him if he's scheduled his vasectomy yet, if not, no sex.

201) Gag at the mention of a blowjob.

202) Tell him his back hair is a major turn-off and he'll just have to shave before you can get in the mood.

203) Mention that you've noticed he may have the early signs of erectile dysfunction and tell him you've left a message for his physician to call him for an appointment as soon as possible.

204) Ask him if he wants you to be conscious of his premature ejaculation issue tonight.

205) Give him a Hustler® magazine and
tell him to take care of it himself.

206) Read a transvestite magazine... note the usual caution.

207) Strap on a dildo and tell him you
want to try something "different" tonight.

208) Rig a Magic 8 Ball® to always show the words
"NO,"
"NOT TONIGHT,"
or
"DON'T EVEN THINK ABOUT IT."

209) Tell him you want to have
a romantic movie night and
slip in Brokeback Mountain...

210) FREE PASS

211) Give him a blow-up doll to use, but make it a male.

212) If he likes the alternate hole, tell him,
"What's good for the goose..."

213) Serve Chinese food for dinner and stuff
a fortune cookie with a slip of paper saying,

"DO NOT expend any energy in bed tonight,
you'll need it all tomorrow. Just wait... you'll see why."

214) If your man has gray pubic hair, bring
a bottle of Grecian® Formula 16® into bed and
tell him you really need to spray that area
before you can get turned on.

215) Ask him if you can spray paint his bald spot first.

216) Slap on a pair of Laughing Venus™ underwear, hop into bed, and point to the graphic stating, "Do Not Enter."

CHAPTER 6
PHYSICAL BARRIERS

Physical barriers are an effective way to buy a free night.

Here are some suggestions to get your
creative juices going (and not those other juices).

217) Night one:
Let one of your kids sleep between you
because they need Mama.

218) Night two:
Let child #2 sleep between you "just to be fair."

219) Night three:
Let the dog sleep between you so he doesn't feel left out.

220) Sleep in a full body wetsuit to
stretch it out for summer.

221) Go to bed in a sleeping bag.

222) Put a full body pillow in between you and your partner, use Velcro® to attach it to the bed if needed.

223) Place that male blow-up doll between you and your partner in bed.

224) Find an old antique chastity belt, try it on before bed, lock it, and lose the key.

PHYSICAL BARRIERS

225) Find your man a job he has to travel for...
all the time.

226) Sleep in tight jeans and tell him
you need to stretch them out for a
fat friend who wants to borrow them tomorrow.

227) Tell your man you need to sleep
with your child tonight, as he is having nightmares.

CHAPTER 7
VINTAGE EXCUSES

We've all used these timeless excuses.

Sometimes they work and
sometimes you meet resistance.

Throw them in every once in a while
for maximum effect.

228) I have a headache.

229) We just did it last night.

230) I'm beat.

231) I forgot to take my pill.

232) I can feel an aura coming on for a migraine.

233) We're out of condoms.

234) We'll do it tomorrow.

235) I have PMS, so don't even ask.

236) I have lower back pain and am
worried I will get a herniated disc.

237) I have a really stiff neck and
can barely move.

238) I have a stomachache and
need to sit on the toilet.

239) I feel bloated.

240) FREE PASS

241) I've decided to be a
"born again virgin."

CHAPTER 8
SPECIAL SITUATION EXCUSES (SSE)

GENERAL DAY-TO-DAY SSE

Take advantage of these golden times in your life
to throw out situation related excuses.

242) On Mother's Day — a sex-free night
should be part of your gift.

243) On your birthday — you deserve to
relax and call the shots.

SPECIAL SITUATION EXCUSES (SSE)

244) On your child's birthday — giving birth
to the kids was exhausting enough.
You're entitled to recoup your energy today.

245) Fell off your diet — you already have
enough mental stress to deal with.

246) Botched cosmetic procedure

247) Any negative comment from your man
regarding your appearance —
automatic "no sex" night.

248) On the day you have to shop for swimsuits —
you've seen enough of your body that day.

249) The scale is up five pounds —
you're too disgusted with your body to have sex.

PREGNANCY RELATED SSE

Simply tell him...

250) Your water broke or
you may have just peed the bed.

251) The baby's head has dropped and he might poke it.

252) You're contracting and can't deal
with anything else that's "hard" right now.

253) You both need to get your sleep
before the baby comes.

254) You feel nauseous and will puke if you move.

SPECIAL SITUATION EXCUSES (SSE)

255) You feel like he might crush the baby.

256) FREE PASS

257) If he as much as looks at your breasts,
they hurt — so don't even think
about coming near you.

258) You just applied hemorrhoid and
stretch-mark creams.

259) You feel too ugly due to your
"mask of pregnancy." Use makeup to
enhance your mask so that
you resemble a raccoon.

260) You're contracting so hard,
it just may snap his penis off.

261) FREE PASS

262) The doctor just told you that
you may have sextuplets.

CAUTION: Use of the word sex in any context is risky.

263) You just had a prenatal check up and
were already poked there once today.

264) Sex may cause you to dilate,
go into premature labor, be bedridden,
and then you'd need to hire
someone to take care of you,
the kids, the house, meals, laundry, etc.

Is he willing to risk it?

BIRTH RELATED SSE

265) Breast feed in bed.

266) Ask him to check at your episiotomy
to see if it's healing.

267) Tell him your nipples are
too sore from breast-feeding.

268) Continue to wear your big mesh underpants
with a large pad that you got from
the hospital after giving birth.

269) FREE PASS

MENOPAUSAL RELATED SSE

Simply state...

270) I'm dry as dirt down there and
may scratch your penis.

CAUTION: Friction is sometimes what he's after.

271) I feel way too bloated and can't have
any pressure on my abdomen.

272) I have menopausal related osteoporosis and don't want to risk breaking a bone.

273) My nightgown is wet and I'm not sure if it's hot flashes or incontinence.

274) If you touch me you'll send me into a hot flash.

"Tell your man you've decided to pick up the guitar..."
(EXCUSE #172)

HOLIDAY RELATED SSE

Do the following:

NEW YEAR'S EVE

275) Stall until he's asleep by making a list of all the men you kissed at the strike of midnight over the years.

SPECIAL SITUATION EXCUSES (SSE)

276) Drink too much and pass out.

277) Drink too much and wet yourself.

EASTER

278) Tell him you need to hide the Easter eggs...

279) or fill the Easter baskets...

SPECIAL SITUATION EXCUSES (SSE)

280) or refuse to entertain the option
due to how early you have to get up
for Easter sunrise service.

281) FREE PASS

FOURTH OF JULY

282) Pretend you can't hear him request sex
because you're hearing impaired
from the fireworks display.

283) Stall until he's asleep by dying your pubic hair
red, white, and blue for the holiday.

CAUTION: This may turn him on.

YOM KIPPUR

284) Tell him you're too weak from fasting.

HALLOWEEN

285) Tell him you need to sew the Halloween costumes...

286) or bake the pumpkin seeds for
the kids snack tomorrow...

287) or you're too tired from trick or treating...

288) or you're too scared...

289) or explain to him that you're too bloated
from all of the candy you hand picked
out of your kids Halloween buckets and ate.

LABOR DAY

290) Tell him you couldn't possibly have sex tonight because Labor Day will always remind you of your labor and birth experiences with the kids and how traumatic it was.

THANKSGIVING

291) Keep your eyes shut, lay motionless, and complain that the tryptophan in the turkey made you so drowsy you can't even move.

292) Casually mention that you
need to get to sleep early and
save your energy for the
after-Thanksgiving sale tomorrow.

293) Tell him you're bloated
from the three pieces of pie
(pumpkin, apple and pecan)
that you ate for dessert and
you need to sleep it off.

CHRISTMAS

294) Tell him you need to wrap the Santa gifts...

295) or you need to load the Christmas music on the IPod®...

296) or you're too stressed out by the sheer amount of money you've spent on gifts...

297) or you're holding out to see
how good your Christmas gift is first...

298) or you drank too much eggnog and ate too many
Christmas cookies to think about having sex.

299) Since the malls are open until midnight,
stay until close.

HANUKKAH

300) Tell him you are too full
from all of the latkes you ate...

301) or too tired from
spinning the dreidel all night.

CHAPTER 9
EMERGENCY DIVERSION TECHNIQUES

Sometimes, one must resort to drastic measures.

That's where Emergency Diversion Techniques
come into play.

302) Roll out of bed, gently hit your head,
cross your eyes, and tell him
you're worried about a concussion.

303) Fake Turrets Syndrome — start yelling
obscene words out of the blue.

CAUTION: Don't use the words "fuck" or "screw you"!

304) Pre-record a kid's crying tone on your cell phone and hit this "emergency" button.

305) Cough up a hairball.

(TOP #19 — hair from your hairbrush. Roll it up into a ball and hold in your palm)

306) Start an argument.

307) Invite your single girlfriend over
for a movie night and slumber party.

CAUTION: Need we spell it out?

308) Pre-record your house security alarm on
your cell phone and hit this "emergency" button.

309) Set your pager to go off and
pretend you have an urgent work call.

310) Dribble some cherry juice under your nose and on the sheets to cause a "never ending" nosebleed.

311) Flirt with the nearest male.

312) Pre-record the neighbors fighting on your cell phone and hit this "emergency" button.

313) Pick a poison ivy leaf and rub the essence
on the inside of your man's underwear.

314) Rub nectar on your man's penis and
set a bee free under the covers.

315) Pre-record glass breaking on
your cell phone and hit this "emergency" button.

Request that he go downstairs to check it out.

316) Have a voodoo doll made of your man and poke him between the legs before bed.

317) Scream at your man,
"YOU'RE NOT GETTING SEX TONIGHT!"

318) Play dead.

CHAPTER 10
NEVER DO THIS

Sometimes preventing arousal is the best tactic.

Here are a number of things to keep in mind
to avoid igniting the sexual spark.

NEVER... NEVER... NEVER

319) Make any reference to boob, breast, tits,
teat, jugs, nipple, boobies, or headlights.

320) Mention penis, cock, dick, shaft, meat, or wank.

321) Say words relating to supple, hard, or stiff.

322) Look succulent when going to bed.

323) Wear sexy negligees, lingerie, thong underwear, fishnet stockings, garter belts, shiny lipstick, push-up bras, g-strings, stiletto heels, or short skirts.

324) Have visible massage gels, lotions, or K-Y® Jelly.

325) Show any nipple or breast tissue (even 1/20 of a millimeter of breast tissue is a turn-on to men).

326) Make any reference to the following sexual toys: vibrating bullet, pocket rocket, or g-spot vibrator.

327) Say the words panty or bra.

328) Make any promises with respect to future sex — he'll remember and remind you forever.

329) Allow any part of your body to touch any part of his body, even a toe.

330) Get a Brazilian pubic wax.

331) Reference any fruits including cherry, melon, or peach and don't eat a banana in the bedroom.

332) Watch a TV show in the bedroom
that may have a sex scene.

333) Display titillating magazines or catalogs.

334) Allow any whipped cream into the bedroom.

335) Go to bed naked.

336) Purchase flavored lubricants.

337) Undress in front of him.

338) Talk about your yoga session or
say the phrase "downward dog."

339) Allow anything that resembles
a pole in the bedroom.

340) Say the words lick, kiss, tongue, or suck.

341) Bend over.

342) In fact, don't even enter the bedroom!

NEVER TO APHRODISIACS

Aphrodisiacs are named after Aphrodite,
the Greek goddess of sexual love and beauty.

These nasty little encouragers should not come
in contact with your man under any circumstances.

343) Oysters — When ordering an appetizer, have the calamari instead. Making a stew? Stick with clam chowder.

CAUTION: Clam is another word you should never mention!

344) Onions — Just use a lot of salt and pecker,
I mean pepper, to spice up your burgers.

345) Garlic — If your man has garlic breath,
it's not a good thing — find a quick excuse!

Some clinicians have even suggested crushing garlic and
rubbing it on the penis as an aphrodisiac.

Don't ever let your husband rub garlic on his penis!

346) Beans — You know the added benefit of keeping these away from your husband.

347) Malunggay tea — Some sources say that drinking boiled malunggay tea leaves is better than Viagra®!

348) Stay away from the blood or meat of the
Philippine cobra which is known to be one of
the most venomous and dangerous snakes in the world
and is also believed to be a very good aphrodisiac.

349) Rhinoceros horns and penis —
especially applicable to women whose husbands
have brought back a mounted rhino
from an African safari.

350) And... if your husband is an African safari kind of guy, beware that certain tiger parts such as the penis, bones, fat, and liver are still being used to make a powerful aphrodisiac soup.

If he lands a tiger, only the animal's hide is allowed in the house!

What's up with animal penis increasing sex drive? Are all male species the same?

351) Betel nuts — areca nuts are seeds of the
areca palm tree growing in most tropical countries.

These are also known as betel nuts because
they are mostly chewed with the betel leaf.
This leaf has a peppery taste.

Don't ever let your man
shimmy up the areca palm tree while on
vacation and pick the nut!

If he's a gourmet cook, make sure he's not
substituting betel for pepper in his favorite recipes!

352) Never cook with the following herbs or spices:
cayenne pepper, cardamom, cinnamon, clove,
garlic, mace, nutmeg, parsley, or basil... bland is best!

353) Take out all of the green M&M's®,
you can never be too safe!

CHAPTER 10

NEVER BE HOME

..as no tactics will work when:

354) He returns from fishing, hunting or any other trips to the wilderness.

355) He returns from a guy trip to Vegas.

356) He gets home after a stag party.

CHAPTER 11
TIMES TO SUGGEST SEX

EXPERT LEVEL ONLY
*** CAUTION ***

Sometimes, the best defense is a good offense.

In this section, we are creating as many
moments as possible where you are asking for sex
(even begging and pleading).

The goal is to ask when you are virtually guaranteed
to be turned down, resulting in several occasions
to point back to when you are using the
tactics provided in the previous sections.

"I remember the night when... and you
turned me down. I'm not trying to weasel out of sex,
our timing is just off. Damn."

THROW IT OUT THERE...

357) During the Super Bowl, Masters Tournament, Final Four, Olympics, Stanley Cup, or World Series.

358) After he's up, showered, dressed, heading out the door to work, and running late for his performance review.

359) Right in the middle of an outdoor yard work or garage cleaning project.

360) As he is heading out to play golf.

361) Right after you get back from a long run or workout session and you're dripping wet and smelly.

362) During an intense video game your sweetie is playing.

363) When you know guests will be
arriving any minute.

364) Right before he heads out to do his
Ironman® triathalon.

365) Right after he gets home from his vasectomy.

And there you have it...

An entire years worth of new, unique and
outrageous ways to weasel your way out of sex on those
nights that your desire is to sleep instead of romp.

And remember, if you do end up giving in...
negotiate a little "treat" into the deal!

Media and press have coined authors
Addie Michel and Marie Chablis
the "humorous" sexperts.

Their love of friendship and laughter sparked a creative
partnership that lead to their newly released book,
Not Tonight Darling, I Have A Headache!
365 Ways to Weasel Your Way Out of Sex.

ABOUT MARIE CHABLIS

Marie Chablis has worked as a nurse practitioner
as well as a researcher in the medical industry
for the last 15 years. She has published on numerous
scientific topics in journals and text books.

She currently works in research development for
a biotech company and is co-owner of Laughing Venus.

She has been happily married for 13 years and
has 2 young children.

ABOUT ADDIE MICHEL

Addie Michel enjoyed 19 successful years in sales and marketing before unleashing her creative side with a second career in the children's fashion world.

She is now co-owner of Laughing Venus and has been happily married for 19 years.

She considers herself a "not so" stay-at-home mom with 3 young children.

Addie and Marie believe in sharing humor,
enjoying relationships and living on the light side of life.

To secure Marie and Addie for your next speaking
engagement, contact them at info@laughingvenus.com.
They promise to provide an inspirational and
humorous presentation.

Printed in the United States
221917BV00002B/5/P